WALKING WITH HENRY

THE LIFE AND WORKS OF HENRY DAVID THOREAU

THOMAS LOCKER

Fulcrum Publishing
Golden, Colorado

The Thoreau Institute at Walden Woods
Lincoln, Massachusetts

Once there was a nature writer

Named Henry David Thoreau

Who lived in Concord, Massachusetts,

And loved to walk in the wilderness.

One day Henry

Cut down a sapling for a walking stick.

Leaving the cares of civilization behind

He followed a path by the river.

The path ended at the edge of the wilderness.

Henry set up his tent and

Peeled the bark from his walking stick

As the lingering sunset faded and

Darkness covered the land.

At first light, he entered the pathless wilderness.

The air was filled with the smells of plants

Growing and decaying.

Listening to the sounds of animals,

Henry studied the moss and the ferns, the trees and the flowers,

Walking carefully to avoid snakes.

The farther he went from civilization,

The happier he became.

At the top of a waterfall, Henry took out

His knife and whittled his stick.

Time seemed to disappear.

Later, startled by the hooting night owls,

Henry sat up in his tent, then fell asleep

Listening to the sound of falling water.

When he awoke, the grass was covered with

Morning dew. It looked like a mirror

Broken into a thousand fragments

Wildly reflecting the full blaze of the rising sun.

Through the glare and mist, Henry was

Astonished to see a large moose

Entering the forest.

Hoping for a closer look,

Henry followed the moose tracks.

They led to a sparkling lake

At the foot of a gigantic mountain.

It was like a dream of paradise.

He wondered what he would see

From the mountaintop.

Using his sturdy walking stick,

Henry struggled up the mountain

Passing huge rocks that seemed to

Have been dropped from an unseen quarry.

Bone tired, Henry reached the summit

As the last light of day faded into night.

The moon rose silently, and

Millions of stars appeared in the endless sky.

Huddling close to the warmth

Of his small crackling campfire

Henry carved the handle of his staff

Until it fit perfectly in his hand.

At dawn Henry picked up his stick.

It wasn't too short or too long.

It wasn't too thick or too thin.

Like the wilderness, it was the way it should be.

Henry looked out over the world

And then descended into the rising mist.

As he started home, the woods became dark.

Trees began to sway in a wild, howling wind.

Henry heard the fierce drumbeat of

Rain pounding on the roof of the forest.

Soon both Henry and the wilderness were soaked.

When the storm ended, everything became silent.

A brown wood thrush sang and another answered.

Henry listened to the sound of the creek filling

And recognized familiar rocks, trees, and animals.

It was like meeting old friends or even family.

Enjoying the fellowship, Henry sauntered

Toward the light streaming in from

The edge of the wilderness.

The warm sun on his back

Was like a gentle herdsman leading him home.

When he found the path by the river,

His heart was filled with a love of the world.

Near his home, he planted an acorn in case

He would ever need another walking stick.

But his walking stick, shaped and tested

By the wilderness, lasted for many years.

The acorn grew into a wild and noble oak, and

Henry David Thoreau's words about wildness

Still echo across the land.

MILESTONES

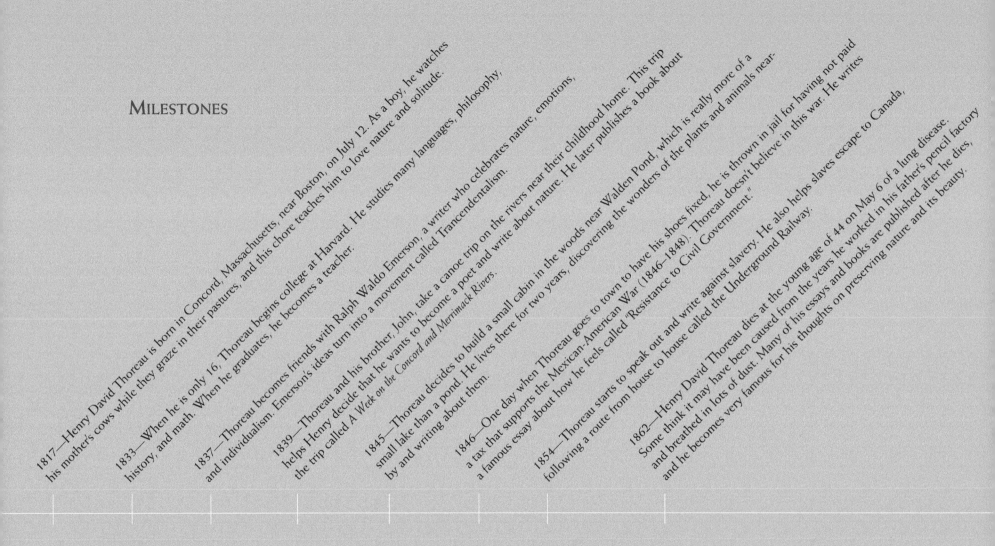

1817—Henry David Thoreau is born in Concord, Massachusetts, near Boston, on July 12. As a boy, he watches his mother's cows while they graze in their pastures, and this chore teaches him to love nature and solitude.

1833—When he is only 16, Thoreau begins college at Harvard. He studies many languages, philosophy, history, and math. When he graduates, he becomes a teacher.

1837—Thoreau becomes friends with Ralph Waldo Emerson, a writer who celebrates nature, emotions, and individualism. Emerson's ideas turn into a movement called Trancendentalism.

1839—Thoreau and his brother, John, take a canoe trip on the rivers near their childhood home. This trip helps Henry decide that he wants to become a poet and write about nature. He later publishes a book about the trip called *A Week on the Concord and Merrimack Rivers*.

1845—Thoreau decides to build a small cabin in the woods near Walden Pond, which is really more of a small lake than a pond. He lives there for two years, discovering the wonders of the plants and animals nearby and writing about them.

1846—One day when Thoreau goes to town to have his shoes fixed, he is thrown in jail for having not paid a tax that supports the Mexican-American War (1846–1848). Thoreau doesn't believe in this war. He writes a famous essay about how he feels called "Resistance to Civil Government."

1854—Thoreau starts to speak out and write against slavery. He also helps slaves escape to Canada, following a route from house to house called the Underground Railway.

1862—Henry David Thoreau dies at the young age of 44 on May 6 of a lung disease. Some think it may have been caused from the years he worked in his father's pencil factory and breathed in lots of dust. Many of his essays and books are published after he dies, and he becomes very famous for his thoughts on preserving nature and its beauty.

Henry David Thoreau was born on July 12, 1817, in Concord, Massachusetts, where he spent most of his life. From childhood, he loved nature, and as a young adult, decided to dedicate his life to studying and writing about the world around him. In later years, his love of plants and animals extended to a dedication to the rights of his fellow man, particularly African Americans. Though Thoreau died at a young age, his writings are still studied and cherished today, nearly 200 years after his death.

HENRY DAVID THOREAU WAS A WALKER WHO SPENT SEVERAL HOURS EACH DAY WANDERING IN THE WOODS. WHEN HE RETURNED FROM HIS WALKS, HE WROTE SOME OF THE FINEST THINGS EVER WRITTEN ABOUT NATURE. HERE ARE A FEW SELECTIONS OF HIS WORDS.

"We need the tonic of wildness…we can never have enough of Nature."

"The world is but a canvas to our imaginations."

"I seek acquaintance with Nature, to know her moods and manners."

"In short, all good things are wild and free."

"I think that I cannot preserve my health and spirits, unless I spend four hours a day at least…sauntering through the woods and over the hills and fields, absolutely free from all worldly engagements."

"In the society of many men, or in the midst of what's called success, I find my life of no account, and my spirits rapidly fall…But when I have only a rustling oak-leaf, or the faint metallic cheep of a tree sparrow, for variety in my winter walk, my life becomes continent and sweet as the kernel of a nut."

"A man is rich in proportion to the number of things which he can afford to let alone."

"Regard man as an inhabitant, or a part and parcel of Nature, rather than a member of society."

Dedicated to my son, Greg, the first walker
of the Appalachian Trail from Georgia to Maine
in the year 2000.

Library of Congress Cataloging-in-Publication Data

Locker, Thomas, 1937–
Walking with Henry : based on the life and works of Henry David
Thoreau / Thomas Locker.
p. cm.
Summary: Introduces philosopher, writer, and environmentalist Henry
David Thoreau, using selections from his own writings and an imaginary
journey into the wilderness.
ISBN 978-1-55591-355-7 (Hardcover)
ISBN 978-1-55591-016-7 (Paperback)
1. Thoreau, Henry David, 1817–1862—Juvenile literature. 2.
Wilderness areas—Juvenile literature. 3. Walking—Juvenile literature.
4. Nature—Juvenile literature. [1. Thoreau, Henry David, 1817–1862. 2.
Authors, American. 3. Naturalists. 4. Wilderness areas. 5. Walking. 6.
Nature.] I. Title.
PS3053 .L58 2002
818'.309—dc21

2002003881

Printed in the United States

0 9 8 7 6 5 4 3 2

Design by Nancy Duncan

Fulcrum Publishing
4690 Table Mountain Drive, Suite 100, Golden, Colorado 80403
800-992-2908 • 303-277-1623
www.fulcrumbooks.com

The Thoreau Institute at Walden Woods
Lincoln, Massachusetts